# THE Μετάνοία Method Handbook

**The Companion Guide To**
***The Metanoia Method: How The Brain, Body, And Bible Work Together***

Mind Change, LLC

Written and Created by Kent & Heather McKean



Printed in the United States of America



All Greek and Hebrew words and definitions are from Bible Hub, unless otherwise notated.

*Medical Disclaimer* — The contents of this work are based on personal experiences, research conducted by the authors (unless otherwise noted), and experiential data collected from work with clients. The authors present this information for educational purposes only. Concerning the complex and highly individualized nature of any health problem, this book and the ideas, methods, procedures, and suggestions herein are not intended to replace the advice of trained medical professionals. All matters regarding an individual's physical or mental health require medical supervision. A medical professional should be consulted prior to adopting any program, programs, or methods described in this book or any information shared by the Mind Change Institute® and its affiliate programs. The authors disclaim any liability arising directly or indirectly from the use of this book. Anyone reading this book or using methods suggested in this book acknowledges that they have read and understood the details of this disclaimer and take complete responsibility for the outcome of any implementation of the material herein.

Mind Change, LLC
PO Box 791377
Paia, HI 96779

www.MindChange.com

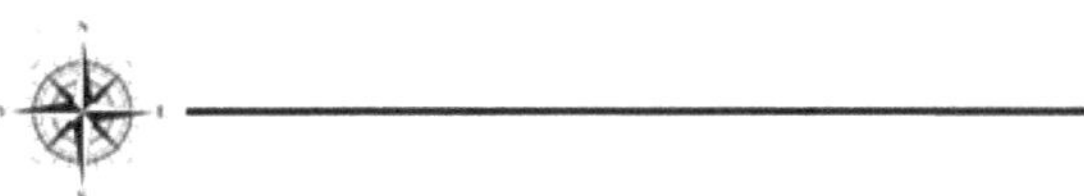

# TABLE OF CONTENTS

# INTRODUCTION

*"Do not conform to the pattern of this world, but be transformed by the renewing of your mind."*
*Romans 12:2*

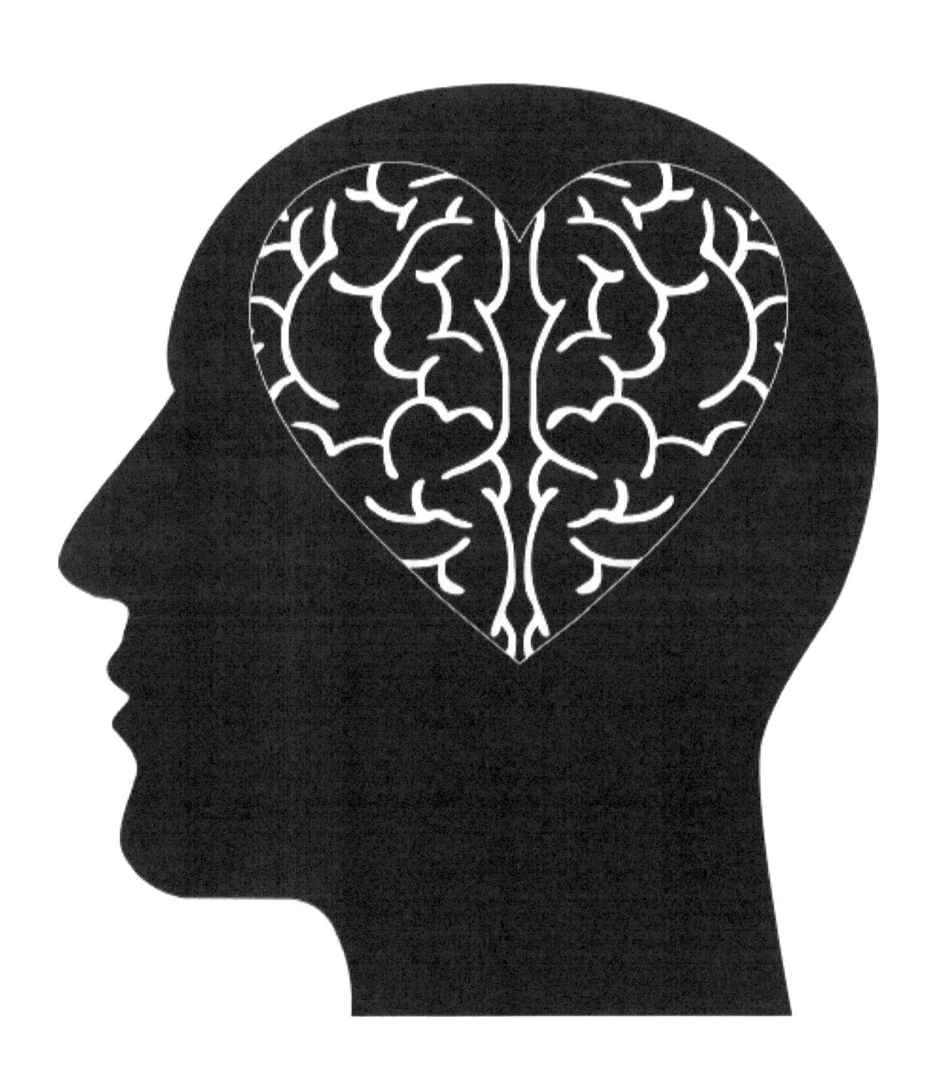

Welcome to *The Metanoia Method Handbook* – a Companion Guide. Congratulations on investing in the most powerful resource of all: YOUR MIND! The journey within is not for the faint-hearted, so I have provided this book to support you as you embark on this great adventure.

One of the most prominent overarching themes to "self-work" is almost always: Love. Love yourself enough to take the time and energy to invest in this process. AND, be loving to yourself in the process.

Remember, the things you want to change are a result of subconsciously "practicing" them for years, decades or generations! Some of these things may have been passed down over centuries. Transforming your mind about your problem, life, or disease takes considerably less time to change than it did to build, but still, give yourself the time and space to do so. And transformation is at the heart of repentance, core to the gospel of Christ!

Metanoia Method is not for the timid. It is for the brave. The few people ready to "take on" everything they think they know and turn it upside down will tap into a power that they only dreamed possible. The hardest and best knowledge we must face is that we have a choice, and this choice is given to us by God. It is a gift!

*As Jesus went on from there, two blind men followed him, calling out, "Have mercy on us, Son of David!"*

*When he had gone indoors, the blind men came to him, and he asked them, "Do you believe that I am able to do this?"*

*"Yes, Lord," they replied.*

*Then he touched their eyes and said, "According to your faith let it be done to you"*

*Matthew 9:27-29*

In the following chapters, we will lay out a step-by-step plan to help you transform your mind. This handbook will cover the following:

### Metanoia Manifesto

This will help you identify exactly what you would like to see in your future so that you can know where you are going. This is arguably the MOST important step of the Metanoia Method process!

### Metanoia GPS

This will be your "directions" and tools to get you where you are going. We will teach you how to utilize your Gratitude, Positive Affirmations, and Smiles (Happy Memories) to begin creating your dreams.

### Safe Haven

Having a "safe haven" that we can visit anytime, anywhere, is an extremely valuable tool. Learn how to create and use this technique to help provide a safe place for change.

### PaNE CuRe List

This is a powerful tool that will help you identify the past negative experiences, limiting beliefs, and the programs that are keeping you stuck in some of your unpleasant patterns.

### Pattern Interrupts

Learning this tool, and the power behind it, is a key piece to overcoming the things holding you back.

This guide is based on the tools outlined in *The Metanoia Method: How the Brain, Body and Bible work together.* Specifically, this handbook follows Part 2, and helps you walk through the Metanoia Method. Please review it entirely before attempting to use this guide.

Whether you are working with a practitioner or doing the work on your own, this guide contains tools to complete the process and begin to transform your mind!

This guide is broken down into separate sections with plenty of room to write, draw, post photos, cards, or anything your creative mind can come up with. Each section has a brief summary of the exercise and some prompts to get you started.

For a more detailed and rich understanding of each section, please refer back to Part 2 of *The Metanoia Method*.

Though everyone's journey and timeframe for change will be unique to them, if you apply yourself wholeheartedly to these methods and techniques, they can provide the fastest route to change we have ever encountered.

*"What do you want me to do for you?" Jesus asked him.*
*"Rabbi, I want to see." Mark 10:51*

# LEARNING TO LOVE

To begin this journey, I want to point you to two guiding principles that underlay the foundation of this work. You may recognize them as the 2 Greatest Commandments from Mark 12:30-31:

- *Love the Lord your God with all your heart and with all your soul and with all your mind and with all your strength.*

- *Love your neighbor as yourself.*

It is our belief that Jesus had a very good reason for summing up the the Law and the Prophets into these two commandments. So let's do a brief overview of the main concepts behind these principles.

> *"Love the Lord your God with all your heart and with all your soul and with all your mind and with all your strength."*

**Heart**—(Hebrew word *leb* (לֵבָב), Greek word *Kardia* (καρδία)) – the heart, mind, character, inner self, will, intention, center that governs our somatic, mental, and emotional attributes. And although we typically relate the heart to emotions, the Bible's intention of the word is related primarily to our thoughts.

**Soul**—(Hebrew word *nephesh* (נֶפֶשׁ) Greek word *Psuché* (ψυχή)) – the breath of life, the soul as the seat of emotions, individuality; it is the direct aftereffects of God breathing his
gift of life into a human being.

**Mind** — (Greek word *Dianoia* (διάνοια)) – the mind, disposition, thought, understanding, intellect, insight.

**Strength** — (Hebrew word *meod* (מְאֹד), Greek word *Ischus* (ἰσχύς)) – absolute strength, power, might, force, ability.

In this passage, we have God helping us understand, from the beginning, that we were created to have congruency and wholeness is all of these areas of our being: heart, soul, mind, and strength.
There is a distinguishable flow in this teaching: Everything stems from our inner self, our thought life (heart), and then overflows into the outer self, the emotions and desires and passions we let drive us (soul). This creates the filters, perceptions, and personal model of the world (mind).

Finally, we find the outcome of our choices, desires, and thoughts in the fruit of our life (strength). How easily we fragment our whole being. The reason that this was (and still is) the Greatest Commandment is, the only way we are going to be able to make it through the sin, lies, and hardship of this human experience, is to realize just how darn lovable we actually are! God is asking us to give Him our EVERYTHING, for the simple reason of desiring to cleanse each area of our lives in which we have *deviated* away from His abundant love. If we can understand and internalize the first commandment, the second will come quite naturally!

*"Love your neighbor as yourself."*

Don't believe me? That's fine. Take it from an 18th century theologian and Biblical scholar named John Gill, whose commentary work is now used by some of the top theologians around today. Listen to what he says about this command in *John Gill's Exposition of the Bible*:

> *"This law supposes, that men should love themselves, or otherwise they cannot love their neighbour..."* [1]

There you have it! We need to love ourselves. It isn't "selfish". It isn't "sinful". It's a command. In fact, it's one of the Greatest Commands. One of two. Sounds pretty important to me. Far be it from me to try to reinvent the wheel when it comes to spiritual enlightenment. I feel pretty confident that Jesus knew what He was talking about. A book that I love and highly recommend is, *God Loves Me and I Love Myself,* by Mark DeJesus. In his book, the author goes into great detail regarding the destructive Christian narrative that self-love is sinful. I would like to include a passage from this book below to help focus our thoughts on this subject:

*"My biggest challenge in working with people is helping them see the problem that is driving the spider web of issues in their lives. Deep down, the battle has to do with how they process love for themselves. It manifests in every area of their life, affecting how they do life and relationships, but they often don't see the connection….*
*In my calling of helping people overcome, I have found a lack of self-love tops the charts on the list of battlegrounds they face. I believe we cannot avoid it much longer. God is leading us to face this issue in a heart to heart manner so that our land can experience the needed healing. Here's the problem. I am pinpointing a subject most people do not even have a reference for. I am addressing a need most people didn't even know they carried. We all want to be loved, but we were never taught the importance of loving ourselves the way God loves us. That's why I believe this book could save your life.*

**WHAT I AM NOT SAYING**

*Before you come up with your own conclusions, allow me to explain what true self-love is in its purest form, by first explaining what self-love is not. I would hate to begin on a faulty definition or perspective. Because this topic is alien to most, allow me to bring clarification by showing you what self-love is not.*

## 1. Self-centered

*Focusing solely on one's self with little regard for others, has nothing to do with self-love and is more self-idolatry. Selfishness and self-centeredness are counterfeits that are not concerned with loving others authentically, but elevating one's self. True love says, I am willing to lay down my life for another. Those who are narcissistic are not operating from the heart of true self-love. They live what is often referred to as an ego-centric reality, where life to them is all about themselves. Narcissists find ways to remain in a selfish world that is vain, spending very little time thinking or empathizing over others. Many who say they love themselves are often typical narcissists because they make most situations, conversations and scenarios circle back to themselves. Their emphasis always seems to be what's going on with them, their viewpoint and their feelings. People who love themselves properly give it out right away. They spend little time obsessing over their own life. Once love is received, it naturally goes out. They have settled love in their hearts, so it flows out very freely.*

## 2. Self-indulgent

*Many times I hear from well-intentioned people who share examples of how they are "loving themselves." Yet they deliver tales of foolish financial decisions and endless hours of wasteful activities, all with a label of self-love. This is not what I am speaking of. Eating a tub of ice cream and checking out with television is not self-love. It's actually a manifestation of lacking self-love, because those experiences do not add life. In fact, those habits can often drive people further into unhealthy emotional prisons.*

1. Matthew 22:39 - meaning and commentary on Bible verse. (n.d.). from https://www.biblestudytools.com/commentaries/gills-exposition-of-the-bible/matthew-22-39.html

### *3. Self-exaltation*

*Years ago, I remember watching someone who was working overtime to draw attention to himself. He went out of his way to make sure people were noticing him. I overheard an observer say, "Well that guy really loves himself." This is a classic mistake. He doesn't. He actually hates himself, but needs extra attention to fill a void in his heart. He exerts extra energy to feel the affirmation of people's eyes observing him. This is not self-love.*

### *4. Self-pity*

*Scores of people live as victims, where their life has been defined by their limitations. This victim mindset has become a modern plague over our generation. Victims become bombarded with problems so much, they find themselves imprisoned by them. Without healthy self-love, they confuse self-pity as a way to comfort themselves. Convinced that no one is showing them love, they seek to comfort themselves by bringing attention to their pain. They see it as comforting themselves, yet it becomes a personal immersion into their problems and woes. Instead of loving on those around, they become isolated in their own trouble, leaving them emotionally unavailable to others. They may think they are "loving themselves" when in reality they are trapped in a prison as victims. This mindset is light-years away from self-love. In fact, self-pity is an absolute counterfeit.*

### *DISCOVERING SELF-LOVE*

*When we truly receive God's love in our hearts, we step into the arena where loving ourselves is possible. The Bible reminds us that we love Him because He first loved us. Father God is the initiator of love. He broadcasts who He is as love to us, with an invitation to love Him back. The fruitfulness of our love relationship with God relies on our hearts receiving the love that is transmitted from heaven. It is imperative to know that loving ourselves is predicated on receiving the unending love that God has for us. We cannot love God until we have first received it from Him and allowed that love to permeate how we see ourselves. The love that God pours out empowers us to see ourselves through that love. Therefore, we can know we have plugged into God's love when we are able to love ourselves properly."* [2]

Hopefully, you can now see how important it is that we accurately assess our own understanding and adherence to the Greatest Commandments. To assist in this process, we have decided to start the next section of this handbook with two exercises that are meant to address our own feelings, beliefs, and possible limitations surrounding these commandments. These exercises alone have the power to completely change the trajectory of your life! Let's dive in.

2. DeJesus, Mark. God Loves Me and I Love Myself!: Overcoming the Resistance to Loving Yourself (p. 16). Kindle Edition.

# VIEW OF GOD

*"Love the Lord your God with all your heart and with all your soul and with all your mind and with all your strength."*

It is our opinion, from personal experience and our work within the ministry and professionally with clients, that many of us have a very distorted view of God. As we discussed, our belief systems start in early childhood and become solidified throughout our lives. The way we view God is distinctly shaped not only by our upbringing, but also by our religious affiliations.

Dr. Andrew Newberg is a doctor of neurotheology—this research applies science and the scientific method to spirituality through brain-imaging studies. These scans have shown how religious practices such as meditation, prayer, or even how we view God can help shape a brain.

Dr. Newberg's research has shown that worshiping a god whom we deem as punitive and distant causes anxiety, depression, and stress. His research also indicates that a fundamentalist form of Christianity (reading the Bible in a strict, legalistic way with a similarly rigid and judgmental mode of practice) damages the brain in ways that are hard to heal. On the flip-side, worshiping a loving, compassionate, and engaging God increases feelings of security, compassion, and love. And the results show that brain function is higher with faster thinking and processing.

The clearer our view of who God is, the perfect God of agape, the more our neuro-circuitry will flow with security and love and compassion, thinking and feeling clearer than ever before. When we have that kind of God-spirit in us, transformation continues to flow. As further proof of God's unconditional love for us, He doesn't ask us to give Him our heart, soul, mind, and strength without having proven *Himself* trustworthy of our love, first. How? Well, the entire Bible is the story of God's effort to regain intimacy with us, which crescendos into the ultimate act of love towards His people… Jesus.

We all *know* the story, but do we let the truth of His abundant love motivate our every thought, word, or deed? In this first exercise, we want you to honestly explore your personal view of God. If you have a warped view of God, you likely have a very good reason. Our goal here is to acknowledge any unloving views that we have placed upon God, and to counteract them with the truth of the Scriptures. Remember, this is no place for guilt, shame, regret, or any other feelings/emotions that might circle you back to unloving thoughts.

Review some of the common *Views of God* below and write any personal "proof" that you have in reference to the associated view:

## Authoritarian God

Very judgmental and engaged. Always watching, waiting for us to mess up or to sin. The best way to stay in his "good graces" is to obey without question, do not doubt, and do everything right with a glad and sincere heart. When things in our life go wrong, it is likely because we are "outside of God's will" and we need to be punished or corrected out of love.

## Critical God

Judgmental but not engaged. He sits on the judgment seat, constantly disappointed in His people. They could never "do enough" or "be enough". They are too worldly, too stubborn, and too sinful. Because His people won't follow the rules, He has decide to sit back and let them suffer their own consequences. His heart is no longer moved by their prayers. No-one is worthy of His presences, grace, or mercy.

## Distant God

Completely removed from His Creation. Though He may have once engaged with His people, God no longer has any involvement with us. He no longer engages in the battle and leaves His people to wrestle with their own interpretation of the Law. He has abandoned the Earth and given up on His people because they kept going astray.

## Benevolent God

Judgmental and very engaged. Intimately involved in our creation and interested in our unique purpose. Desiring intimacy, honesty, and open communication with His children. Trusts His children to make good choices and encourages them to live a full life, full of freedom. Understanding that His children live in a world that will pull at their hearts, minds, and souls, He is constantly working for their good and ready to listen and provide support if they should want it. He does not interfere without permission and sees the best in every being.

## My Current View of God

Take this opportunity and space to talk about your personal view of God. Do not hold back or "edit" here. This exercise can be very revealing and provide you with helpful feedback about your personal walk with God. This is the place to include some of those pesky little thoughts/feelings/emotions/doubts or voices in your head.

## My DESIRED View of God

Take this opportunity and space to use your faith and imagination. If you could create your ideal view of God, making it the BEST of the BEST, what would you like to believe about God? How would He view you? What would a relationship with this God be like for you?

*"You are my witnesses," declares the Lord, "and my servant whom I have chosen, so that you may know and believe me and understand that I am he. Before me no god was formed, nor will there be one after me.*

*Isaiah 43:10*

*Yet to all who did receive him, to those who believed in his name, he gave the right to become children of God—*

*John 1:12*

*As for God, his way is perfect: The LORD's word is flawless; he shields all who take refuge in him.*

*Psalm 18:30*

*The LORD is gracious and righteous; our God is full of compassion.*

*Psalm 116:5*

If your personal view of God isn't yet where you would like it to be, or even if it is, we plan on helping you make it *even better*! To do that, we would like to remind you of some of the things that God has said or done to help us understand the truth of His feelings about us.

Remember, the only reason these may be difficult to believe is because you have previous "proof" from your life (and upbringing) that you are using to filter the Scriptures. We will address all of those experiences later in this handbook, but for now, we would invite you to read these statements and respond *AS IF* they are unequivocally TRUE about YOU!

| What God Says About Me | I know this is true because ___________ | How this makes me feel |
|---|---|---|
| *For you created my inmost being; you knit me together in my mother's womb.* **— Psalm 139:13** | | |
| *See, I have inscribed you on the palms of My hands;* **— Isaiah 49:16** | | |
| *Therefore, if anyone is in Christ, he is a new creature. Old things have passed away. Look, all things have become new.* **— 2 Corinthians 5:17** | | |
| *I am fearfully and wonderfully made. Wonderful are your works; my soul knows it very well.* **— Psalm 139:13-14** | | |
| *But you are a chosen people, a royal priesthood, a holy nation, God's special possession, that you may declare the praises of him who called you out of darkness into his wonderful light.* **— 1 Peter 2:9** | | |

| What God Says About Me | I know this is true because ___________ | How this makes me feel |
|---|---|---|
| *For I know the plans I have for you, declares the Lord, plans for welfare and not for evil, to give you a future and a hope.* **— Jeremiah 29:11** | | |
| *Take delight in the Lord, and he will give you the desires of your heart.* **— Psalm 37:4** | | |
| *...for the Lord your God is the One who is going with you. He will not desert you or abandon you.* **— Deuteronomy 31:6** | | |
| *If you believe, you will receive whatever you ask for in prayer.* **— Matthew 21:22** | | |
| *God is acquainted with all my ways. Even before there is a word on my tongue,Behold, Lord, You know it all. You have encircled me behind and in front, And placed Your hand upon me.* **— Psalm 139: 3-5** | | |

# LOVE NOTES

Having a clear, healthy view of God is paramount in our Self-Love journey. Now that you have spent a bit of time understanding the way God feels about you, we can begin to utilize those truths to consider the 2nd Greatest Commandment:

*Love the Lord your God with all your heart and with all your soul and with all your mind and with all your strength.'*

*The second is this: 'Love your neighbor as yourself.'*
*There is no commandment greater than these."*
*Mark 12:30-32*

I have to admit that it has been a bit shocking to realize how many Christians have a hard time with the concept of self-love. The fear of being sel*fish* or *self-absorbed,* is so strong that they are willing to forego (or overlook) the 2nd Greatest Commandment from Jesus. I've heard it said/preached that the second law is "basically saying" that we already love ourselves too much, so we should focus on loving others instead. First off, that is NOT what it says. It says what it says. Love others as you love *yourself.*

I think the problem is *not* that we aren't following this commandment. I think people all over the world *have* been trying to do this. People (especially Christians) will practically kill themselves serving, giving, helping, in an effort to love their neighbor. The real problem is that most of us have not gotten *the first commandment* down yet!!! Why does God command us to love Him with *everything*, first? Is it because He is such a needy God, that He needs to hear how much, or know how much He is loved? *No*! Blasphemy! He doesn't need to know it — *We do*! We need to love Him with everything we have, for the sole purpose of understanding just how much HE. LOVES. US!!! If we get that, the next commandment actually works. We *will* love others like we love ourselves! Because we *do* love ourselves.

I hate to say it, but over the 20+ years that I've been a Christian, I have met more people who "hate" themselves, degrade themselves, beat themselves up, slander themselves, and self-deprecate... and call *that* Christianity. We must to stop this madness. Most of us *do not* love ourselves like God loves us. And we very effectively love our neighbors *just the same* as we love ourselves... terribly!

Should we love others? Of course. But we need to stop listening to the "shame gospel" that continues to beat us up for not giving more of ourselves (when so many are trying to give out of an empty cup), and go back to the first commandment and learn just how darn lovable we a*ctually* are — Lovable enough to *DIE* for.

*For God so loved the world that he gave his one and only son...*
*John 3:16*

*So God created mankind in his own image, in the image of God he created them...*
*Genesis 1:27*

*For you created my inmost being; you knit me together in my mother's womb. I praise you because I am fearfully and wonderfully made; your works are wonderful, I know that full well.*
*Pslam 139:13-14*

The purpose of this exercise is for you to identify your many great qualities and how they benefit you. We are the personalized craftsmanship of our Creator who, incidentally, wants an intimate and close relationship with you.

Do we think God would be okay with, let alone condone, hearing us speak ill of his creation? I think not! If we believe that we are God's Creation, that we are made in His image, knit together in a wonderful way, and worthy of dying for, we should start believing it and living in accordance with that truth.

This Love Notes exercise will help you to focus on your best traits, abilities and talents. You also will come up with ways to practice your strengths in daily life. In doing so, we begin to appreciate and reflect the glory of God's creation... YOU!

# LOVE NOTES EXERCISE

Step 1: Think about the things you love most about yourself. Focus on qualities of your personality that make you unique, strong or lovable. For example:

- **I am: Honest**
- **I am: Brave**
- **I am: Creative**

Now list your positive qualities below:

- **I am:**
- **I am:**
- **I am:**
- **I am:**
- **I am:**
- **I am:**
- **I am:**
- **I am:**
- **I am:**
- **I am:**
- **I am:**
- **I am:**
- **I am:**
- **I am:**
- **I am:**
- **I am:**
- **I am:**

Step 2: Consider the ways in which these qualities have benefited you or someone else in your life. For example:

♥ *The quality of honesty has benefited me because my boss trusts me to work on important projects independently.*

♥ *The quality of bravery has benefited me because I have been able to stand up for what I believe in*

♥ *The quality of creativity has benefited me because I've created artwork that I'm proud to display in my home.*

♥ The quality of has benefited me because:

♥ The quality of has benefited me because:

♥ The quality of has benefited me because:

♥ The quality of has benefited me because:

♥ The quality of has benefited me because:

♥ The quality of has benefited me because:

♥ The quality of has benefited me because:

♥ The quality of has benefited me because:

♥ The quality of has benefited me because:

♥ The quality of has benefited me because:

Step 3: Next come up with ways to honor these qualities in ways that are personally meaningful to you. For example:

- *I will remind myself that I am a good and honest person each day.*
- *When faced with challenges, I will remember the times I have overcome adversity in my life.*
- *I will continue to create because doing so makes me feel more fulfilled and content.*

***Now list the ways you will honor your positive qualities below:***

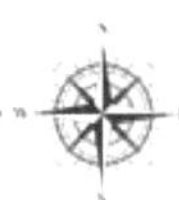

# LOVE MY BODY EXERCISE

Our outward appearance is of little concern to God. 1 Peter 3:3-4 reminds us that our *inner* beauty is of great worth to God. But that doesn't mean that God would be okay with us putting ourselves down or speaking in a derogatory way about our bodies. Remember:

> *Do not let any unwholesome talk come out of your mouths, but only what is helpful for building others up according to their needs, that it may benefit those who listen.*
> *Ephesians 4:29*

Degrading and self-deprecating language is *not* wholesome. Nor it is beneficial, to you or someone who might be listening. Would you let anyone speak about your child in a similar negative way that you speak about yourself? I sure hope not! So please stop speaking that way about God's child, whom He loves and adores, and helped knit together. (That's you!)

Some people may speak ill of their bodies in a way that does not necessarily involve something *outward*, but is still very destructive. When we speak ill of our bodies — "My body is just broke down," "I'm too weak," "I'm too old," "I'm too sick," "I'm broken," etc., we are actually still letting *unwholesome* speech come out of our mouths.

> *This day I call the heavens and the earth as witnesses against you that I have set before you life and death, blessings and curses. Now choose life, so that you and your children may live.*
> *Deuteronomy 30:19*

We need to speak life, love, and blessings over ourselves and our bodies. Our bodies are always *for* us, not against us. Even if our body has resorted to illness or dis-ease, it has done so as a means of communication. It is trying to *tell you something*. We just haven't been taught to listen and have not learned the language of our body. Very few things in this world preform *better* when they are threatened, criticized, berated, and abused. For a short time that behavior might seem to "motivate" but in the long run, you will be worse off. It is time to love our bodies and make peace with them once again. This may take practice and the language may feel "clunky" in the beginning. But we need to persevere in this matter. God was pleased with His Creation. It is time to remember that we are good... *very* good.

**What my body does for me:**

1. ______________________________
2. ______________________________
3. ______________________________
4. ______________________________
5. ______________________________
6. ______________________________
7. ______________________________
8. ______________________________
9. ______________________________
10. ______________________________

**What I love about my body:**

1. ______________________________
2. ______________________________
3. ______________________________
4. ______________________________
5. ______________________________
6. ______________________________
7. ______________________________
8. ______________________________
9. ______________________________
10. ______________________________

**What is unique about me:**

1. ______________________________
2. ______________________________
3. ______________________________
4. ______________________________
5. ______________________________
6. ______________________________
7. ______________________________
8. ______________________________
9. ______________________________
10. ______________________________

**What I can do to take better care of my body:**

1. ______________________________
2. ______________________________
3. ______________________________
4. ______________________________
5. ______________________________
6. ______________________________
7. ______________________________
8. ______________________________
9. ______________________________
10. ______________________________

# MIRROR EXERCISE

*For now we see only a reflection as in a mirror; then we shall see face to face. Now I know in part; then I shall know fully, even as I am fully known*

*1 Corinthians 13:12*

Research into neural activity seems to support the hypothesis that speaking positive affirmations aloud can have a positive impact on self-perception (knowing "in part"). It seems safe to assume that adding a mirror into this practice would only elevate the experience (know "fully"). Many theories within the fields of psychology and neuroscience suggest that mirrors can aid in self-development, helping shift the way we see ourselves, and assist us in grounding into our body.

The mirror has the power to reflect back to you the messages/thoughts/feelings you may have about yourself. This feedback can help make you aware of where you may be resisting and also the areas that are easier for you to accept.

The more you practice the mirror exercise, the more you will begin to release the resistance and become more open to these loving messages. You will learn to connect with yourself on a deeper level than you have done before. For most of us, sitting in front of a mirror and facing ourselves is something we try to avoid. It may be difficult at first, but as you continue, you will become more comfortable with your own reflection.

We recommend that you do this exercise daily for at least 30 days. Though our sincere hope is that this practice becomes a standard part of your self-care regimen. It is our prayer that, as you continue to look into your own eyes day after day, you will begin to see yourself through the eyes of your Father in Heaven (because he sees his amazing and lovable child). For our outward reflection is only a small part of our story. The more you look, the more you will find to love. To know fully, and be fully known.

You will find the steps for the Mirror Exercise on the next page. Feel free to utilize any of your Love Notes, Positive Affirmations, or Love My Body comments as subject matter for your mirror time. You may need to work up to these things. That is okay. Working through the issues that have caused you to not love yourself is not always easy work, but it always worth it. Imagine seeing the world and the people in it through the filter of self-love rather than self-loathing. Learning to love yourself matters because you matter to God.

1. Stand/sit in front of a mirror large enough to see your whole face and body (if possible).

2. Look into your eyes.

3. Take a deep breath and say:
   **"[Your Name], I love you**."

** If this seems too much for you in the beginning, you can say: **"[Your Name] I'm learning to really like you. I'm learning to really love you."**

4. Keep taking deep breaths. Look into your eyes for at least one minute.

5. Throughout the day, each time you pass a mirror or see your reflection, smile and repeat the sentence, even if you have to do it silently.

** Over time, as you become more comfortable with this exercise, you can begin to add your affirmations, Love Notes, and other messages.

# METANOIA MANIFESTO

"Creator" is the first characteristic God reveals to us about himself in Scripture. In the first chapter and verse of Genesis, we are shown who our God is. He is the Creator. God brought to life all things out of nothing. That is how powerful he is, and we are created in his image. We were created in *His* image… to be creators.

Are you resistant to this practice? The fact is that you already do it, probably every day. Are you sick? Every night, you likely go to bed, wondering how you will feel the next morning. You visualize the worst-case scenario. "Will I feel worse? Will a new symptom appear?" You begin to create visual pictures or feelings in your body to represent your tomorrow. You are creating! Good job. But do you like the outcome? No? Change it!

The single most common defense I hear for this type of planning is, "But I don't want to be disappointed when _____ doesn't happen!" Do you hear it? Even the defense is in alignment with what you expect to happen. People feel the need to "be prepared" for the worst. Unfortunately, this usually ends up creating the very thing they say they don't want. Where is faith in this equation? Reconsider these passages with regard to your Manifesto practice:

*Delight yourself in the Lord, and he will give you the desires of your heart.*

*Psalm 37:4 ESV*

*If you abide in me, and my words abide in you, ask whatever you wish, and it will be done for you.*

*John 15:7*

*For everyone who asks receives, and the one who seeks finds, and to the one who knocks it will be opened.*

*Matthew 7:8*

*You do not have, because you do not ask.*

*James 4:2b ESV*

The Metanoia Method Manifesto helps you identify precisely what you would like to see in your future so that you know where you are going. Think of this document as if it holds magical powers. What you write can come true. So don't hold back! This is a story written by you, with details, images, sounds, feelings, and character development. It is a work in progress that can be refined, fine-tuned, and upgraded. It can have pictures, poems, quotes, cards — anything you want that makes you feel good and helps you get a clearer vision of your future. Use words that inspire and are powerfully positive. If you find resistance coming to the surface as you do your Manifesto, that's ok. Just flip over to the Limiting Beliefs Section (p.107) and jot down what comes up. Only include what you DO want in your Manifesto — no negative words allowed. Our words have immense power.

--- REMEMBER ---

*Now to him who is able to do far more abundantly than all that we ask or think, according to the power at work within us,*

*Ephesians 3:20 ESV*

Your Manifesto may include (but is not limited to) the following questions. Take a minute to explore your answers to these questions and jot down what comes up for you.

## Who would I be if I were the best me?

Step out of yourself and see yourself as you'd LIKE to be. This can include character traits, feelings, attributes. If you were the best person you knew, what would you be like?

## What would I do if I succeeded in every venture?

Dare to imagine yourself as a success in everything you do. Try envisioning yourself as a perpetual success. How would this change your dreams?

### How do I choose to serve others and provide value to every relationship?

Giving to others and feeling valued go hand in hand. Create situations that will be a win/win for both parties.

### What relationships do I already have that support and value my vision?

Think about people who “have your back”. Even if they are no longer living, see yourself through their eyes. Notice how they already believe in you and can help you go even further.

### WHAT SKILLS DO I ALREADY POSSESS THAT CAN GET ME CLOSER TO ATTAINING MY GOALS AND OBJECTIVES?

It's a good idea and practice to reflect on your life with the intent of finding tools and skills that you have already attained, and then recognize how you can use those to get even more.

### IF I HAD A MAGIC WAND AND COULD HAVE ANYTHING AND EVERYTHING I DESIRED, WHAT WOULD I HAVE?

Don't limit yourself to tangible ways of achieving things. We will often unknowingly limit ourselves because our reality is so restricted. Allow yourself the freedom to "magically" get things. That way, you can see an unrestricted version of what you want.

## IF I WOKE UP EVERY MORNING FEELING THE BEST I EVER HAVE, WHAT WOULD THAT FEEL LIKE?

Be specific on the visual and "feeling" of this scenario. What would you do if you woke up every day like this? How would your life change?

## WHAT IS GREAT ABOUT MY LIFE NOW AND WHAT WOULD I WANT TO MAKE IT EVEN BETTER?

The power of gratitude cannot be underestimated. This practice alone will make huge strides in feeling better about your life. Taking your gratitude and using it to make more gratitude is an essential life-hack!

### If I had a great and loving childhood, and everyone was doing the best they could, what would it have been like?

This question holds the key to healing so many hurts and pains. Even if you believe you had a horrific childhood, give yourself a moment to see it differently. If your parents really were doing the best job they could (and they likely were, even if it was awful), find some of the wonderful treasures that you may have overlooked in the past. Write a story as if you had the childhood that you wished you had. Be specific about what you would have wanted. Remember, write as if you *already* have it.

## WRITING YOUR MANIFESTO

Now it is time to write your Manifesto. Using some of the information that you wrote in the previous pages, begin to write the story of "where you are going." How you do this is UP TO YOU!! Some people like to do a month-out Manifesto, then a year-out Manifesto, then a 5-year Manifesto, and even a 10-year Manifesto. Don't worry about getting it "just right." You have plenty of time and can re-write the story *even better* whenever you want! This is an organic document. It is meant to be flexible. It will grow and change, just like you! As you start to attract more and more of the things on your list, you will be able to adjust and dream bigger. The only limitations are those that you impose... so don't hold back. When you begin, write this story *as if* it is already happening *now* at a future date of your choice. Here is a sample of how this may begin:

*It is now January 1, 20— and I am feeling amazing. I am surrounded by supportive friends and family and I feel more loved, supported and connected to God than ever before. I am passionate about my work and find purpose in all my endeavors. My body is healthy. I am fit, lean, and strong. Each morning, I wake up early, spend time with God in prayer, meditate on scripture, exercise, and feed my body nutritious food so that I am ready to have an AMAZING day...*

Okay! It's time for you to get started. Have fun and dream big.

*And this is the confidence that we have toward him, that if we ask anything according to his will he hears us. And if we know that he hears us in whatever we ask, we know that we have the requests that we have asked of him.*

*1 John 5:14-15 ESV*

# MANIFESTO

# MANIFESTO

# MANIFESTO

# MANIFESTO

# MANIFESTO

# MANIFESTO

# MANIFESTO

# MANIFESTO

# MANIFESTO

MANIFESTO

# METANOIA GPS

*"Finally my dear brothers and sisters, if you want to cooperate most effectively with God for the healing of your mind, then always choose the truth, hold on to what is honorable, pursue everything that is right and reasonable, practice whatever is healthy, love everything that is pure, embrace whatever is lovely and beautiful, promote whatever is good, and if there is anything that is truly excellent or worthy of praise, fill your minds with such things."*
*Php 4:8 The Remedy Extended Paraphrase*

Now that you have your Metanoia Manifesto, you are clearer on where you are going. Now, you need to recognize the tools you have to get there. This is where the Metanoia GPS comes into play. This GPS gives us all the tools to arrive at our desired destination. What will be included in your GPS?

"G" – GRATITUDE – This can be a daily list of things that you are grateful for. Even entering 5 items every day can be a powerful tool toward getting more of what you want in life.

"P" – POSITIVE AFFIRMATIONS – These can be little quotes, sayings, or purposeful affirmations that are being used to build you up. Rehearse these. Write them daily and read them aloud if possible.

"S" – SMILES – This is ANYTHING that makes you smile! This can be photos, song lyrics, funny little stories, or observations. You can also glue in cards, notes, letters, or other little mementos that bring a smile to your face.

Ideally, this will include happy memories from your past, things you have loved or been inspired by in the past (or present) and will also serve as something you can add to daily. Noticing the blessings about even minor topics can help you reinforce gratitude in your life. Even something as simple as gratitude for the sun streaming through the window can be a powerful practice. Remember, **everything is a skill**. Even happiness!

# GRATITUDE

Gratitude and the "record-keeping" of blessings have been studied and researched for many years. Gratitude builds on itself. Researchers note that daily practice is superior to weekly practice. The brain changes with experience, so the more often gratitude is focused on, the more the brain learns to tune in to the positive things in the world. Though it may take a little extra effort, the payoff can hardly be downplayed. Make an effort to record *at least* 3-5 things you are grateful for daily.

*"Christ has given you peace in your minds. So, let that peace rule your thoughts...Thank God for everything that he gives you."*
*Colossians 3:1 Easy English Bible*

# GRATITUDE

# GRATITUDE

# GRATITUDE

# GRATITUDE

# GRATITUDE

# GRATITUDE

# GRATITUDE

# GRATITUDE

# AFFIRMATIONS

*Life and death are in the power of the tongue.*

*Proverbs 18: 21*

*Therefore my heart is glad and my tongue rejoices; my body also will rest secure.*

*Psalm 16:9*

*Gracious words are a honeycomb, sweet to the soul and healing to the bones.*

*Proverbs 16:24*

Did you know that an affirmation is anything we repeat or affirm? Unfortunately, we *negatively* affirm all of the time. Re-training your mind to affirm *positively* is an incredible tool!

"I AM" are two words that have the power to completely change your life. "I AM" is one of the most powerful phrases we can use. It can be used to empower you or disempower you, so be careful of what you attach to the end of that statement; it will manifest into reality. You already do this in your day-to-day life. When you say "I'm tired", "I'm frustrated", "I'm overwhelmed", you are creating and affirming. Jesus did this, "I AM the way, the truth, and the life, no man comes to the father except through me. I am the vine, you are the branches. I AM the Alpha and the Omega, the beginning and the end. I AM the bread of life. I AM the light of this world. I AM the resurrection of life. I AM THAT I AM!"

Wow! This power was not only given to Jesus, but to His followers as well. We have been given the power to declare, decree, proclaim, and choose life. No other person can say "I AM" for you. Those are words that nobody else can speak over you. You alone have the power and/or authority to use this phrase for your own personal creation. Use them wisely and use them often.

On the next page is a list of common positive beliefs or affirmations. As you begin to identify negative beliefs in later sections, these positive affirmations will be within your grasp and they will become a new and wonderful identity!

# RESPONSIBILITY/SELF-WORTH

I DESERVE LOVE

I AM GREAT AS I AM

I AM HONORABLE

I AM DESERVING

I CAN HAVE _________

I AM SIGNIFICANT

I DESERVE TO LIVE

I DID THE BEST I COULD

I CAN LEARN

I AM A GOOD PERSON

I AM WORTHY

I AM LOVABLE

I DESERVE GOOD THINGS

I CAN BE HEALTHY

I AM INTELLIGENT

I AM OK JUST BEING ME

I DESERVE TO BE HAPPY

I DO THE BEST I CAN

I AM CHOSEN AND HOLY

*Eph 1:4-5 "And he chose us to be his very own, joining us to himself even before he laid the foundation of the universe! Because of his great love, he ordained us, so that we would be seen as holy in his eyes with an unstained innocence."* TPT

I AM COMPLETE

*Col 2:10 "And because you are united with Christ, you are now complete."*

I AM VALUABLE AND LOVED

*Isa 43:4 "You are very valuable to me. you are my special people, and I love you."*

# RELATIONSHIPS

I COMMUNICATE OPENLY WITH OTHERS

I RESOLVE CONFLICTS WITH RESPECT

I SHARE EMOTIONAL INTIMACY WITH OTHERS

I AM THE BEST FRIEND ANYONE CAN HAVE

I CHOOSE FRIENDS WHO LOVE ME THE WAY I AM

THE PEOPLE I LOVE APPROVE OF ME

I AM HAPPY I AM PART OF MY FAMILY

I ENJOY ACTIVITIES AND CELEBRATIONS WITH MY FAMILY

I AM UNCONDITIONALLY LOVED

I AM AN ATTENTIVE MOTHER / FATHER

I COMMUNICATE LOVE AND RESPECT TO MY SPOUSE

I LOVE UNCONDITIONALLY

*Prov 17:17 "A friend loves at all times"*

*1 Pet 4:8 "Above all things, have an intense and unfailing love for one another."*

MY FRIENDSHIPS ARE MUTUALLY BENEFICIAL

*Prov 27:17 "As iron sharpens iron, so one man sharpens another."*

*Prov 27:9 "Perfume and incense bring joy to the heart, and the pleasantness of one's friend springs from his earnest counsel."*

# CONFIDENCE

I AM CONFIDENT, ENTHUSIASTIC, AND ENERGETIC

MY PERSONALITY SHOWS I AM CONFIDENT

I ATTRACT CONFIDENT PEOPLE

I LOVE CHANGE

I EASILY ADJUST TO NEW PEOPLE AND SITUATIONS

I AM OUTGOING AND MAKE FRIENDS EASILY

I AM HAPPY WITH MYSELF THE WAY I AM

I AM PROUD OF MYSELF

MY SELF-ESTEEM AND CONFIDENCE INCREASES EACH DAY

I AM CONFIDENT OF MY SALVATION

*Eph 1:7 "In him we have redemption through his blood, the forgiveness of sins, in accordance with the riches of God's grace."*

I AM STRONG

*Phil 4:13 "I can do all this through him who gives me strength."*

# SAFETY

I AM SAFE

I TRUST MY JUDGEMENT

ALL LIFE LOVES AND SUPPORTS ME

I SAFELY SHOW MY EMOTIONS

ALL IS WELL IN MY WORLD

I MAKE MY NEEDS KNOWN

I FEEL DIVINELY PROTECTED

I AM LOVED

I EASILY LET GO

IT'S OVER NOW

I AM TRUSTED

I AM SECURE

SAFETY SURROUNDS ME

I AM SAFE

*Psalm 18:2 "The Lord keeps me safe. He is my great rock and my strong place."*

*Psalm 46:1 "God, you're such a safe and powerful place to find refuge! You're a proven help in time of trouble - more than enough and always available whenever i need you."*

IT'S OVER NOW

*Isa 43:18 "Forget the former things; do not dwell on the past."*

# SUCCESS

EVERY DAY I BECOME MORE SUCCESSFUL

I FEEL POWERFUL, CAPABLE, AND CONFIDENT

I EASILY FIND SOLUTIONS TO PROBLEMS

MY WORK ENVIRONMENT IS CALM AND PRODUCTIVE

I LOVE LEARNING NEW THINGS AND USING THEM IN MY LIFE

I AM EXPERIENCING WEALTH EVERY DAY

I AM LIVING THE LIFE OF MY DREAMS

I AM FINANCIALLY SUCCESSFUL IN ALL MY ENDEAVORS

I HAVE ALL THE TIME, MONEY, AND LOVE THAT I NEED

GOD WANTS ME TO PROSPER

*3 John 1:2 "Beloved friend, i pray that you may prosper in every way and that you continually enjoy good health, just as your soul is prospering."*

GOD WILL MAKE MY DREAMS COME TRUE

*Psalm 37:4 "Take delight in the Lord, and he will give you the desires of your heart."*

GOD DESIRES FOR ME TO FIND SATISFACTION IN MY LIFE AND WORK

*Ecc 3:12-13 "I know that there is nothing better for people than to be happy and to do good while they live. That each of them may eat and drink, and find satisfaction in all their toil - this is a gift of God."*

# PHYSICAL HEALTH

All my body systems function perfectly

My personality shows I am confident

Every part of my body is healthy and full of energy

I stay healthy and my immune system is very strong

I enjoy strengthening my body with exercise

I feed my body only nutritious food

I pay attention and listen to what my body tells me

I sleep soundly each night, awaking rested and refreshed

I surround myself with healthy people

My body is full of energy and vitality

I am healed by God

*Psalm 147:3 "God heals the broken hearted and binds up their wounds."*

*Jer 14:14 "Heal me Lord, and I will be healed; save me and I will be saved, for you are the one I praise."*

*Jer 33:6 "Nevertheless, I will bring health and healing to it; I will heal my people and will let them enjoy abundant peace and security."*

I sleep with ease

*Psalm 4:8 "In peace I will lie down and sleep, for you alone, Lord, make me dwell in safety."*

# MENTAL HEALTH

ALL OF MY THOUGHTS AND FEELINGS ARE UNDER CONTROL

I AWAKE EACH DAY WITH EXCITEMENT

I AWAIT THE GOOD THINGS COMING TO ME

I BREATHE IN AND OUT, RELEASING ALL STRESS

I EASILY FORGIVE MYSELF AND OTHERS

I OBSERVE MY EMOTIONS WITH PEACE AND GRACE

I MEDITATE WITH JOY AND LOVE

MY THOUGHTS ARE POSITIVE AND UPLIFTING

MY MIND AND BODY ARE PERFECTLY ALIGNED

I FEEL FEELINGS OF LOVE, PEACE, AND JOY

*Psalm 94:19 "When anxiety was great within me, your consolation brought joy to my soul."*

*2 Cor 10:5 "We demolish arguments and every pretension that sets itself up against the knowledge of God, and we take captive every thought and make it obedient to Christ."*

*Isa 43:18 "Forget the former things; do not dwell on the past."*

*John 14:24 "Peace I leave with you; My peace i give to you."*

# POSITIVE AFFIRMATIONS

# Positive Affirmations

# POSITIVE AFFIRMATIONS

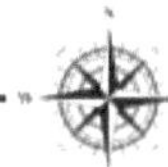

# POSITIVE AFFIRMATIONS

# POSITIVE AFFIRMATIONS

# Positive Affirmations

# Positive Affirmations

# POSITIVE AFFIRMATIONS

# SMILES

This is the section where you will begin to record your Happy Memories! Research suggests that the recalling of positive events can promote mental health resilience. Reminiscing about happy events can increase positive feelings and therefore hinder the release of stress hormones. And remembering the good God has done is a practice highly encouraged throughout the Old and New Testaments!

When I first started my healing journey, I had a very difficult time recalling "a happy memory". I made the assumption that I couldn't find any happy childhood memories because I had a rotten childhood! I was SO wrong. Yes, some not-so-wonderful things happened when I was a child.

But what I eventually realized was that I was representing my entire childhood based on about 18-20 memories that I COULD recall. And they were ALL negative. No wonder I was so miserable. If you remember from *Metanoia Method*, the subconscious mind (where we store memory) is the "Smart Dummy". Meaning that it is highly intelligent because it basically keeps us alive! Regulating our breathing, digestion, heart rate, and so on. But it is "dumb" in the sense that it doesn't "judge." When the subconscious mind is attempting to protect you during difficult times of your life, it will often block out entire *timeframes* or periods of time if it contains a traumatic event.

So if you were 5 years old and had an AMAZING birthday party, full of presents, fun, and love...but then at the very end of the party, you peed in your pants because you were having too much fun to stop and go to the bathroom, what part of this memory are you more likely to hold on to? The part where all your friends (who for the majority of the time were supporting and loving) are now standing around pointing and laughing. Because they are 5 YEARS OLD!!! And pee is funny (when it's not you). The traumatic nature of that event will often result in the subconscious mind "blocking" the majority of the party and focusing in ONLY on the part that makes you feel bad. Why? So that it never happens again.

The result of this kind of mechanism is that we have a much easier time recalling the negative experiences in our life. BUT... we can re-train our brain to get really good at recalling *positive* events from our history. That is an extra gift in this process!

When I finally dealt with a few of the negative memories that I was playing, and replaying FOR YEARS... it unlocked a vault of happy times from my childhood. Amazing, right? The key is: practice makes perfect. That is what the following pages are for. So let's get started!

*"Therefore these stones will always be a memorial for the Israelites."*
*Joshua 4:7b*

*"But Mary treasured up all these things, pondering them in her heart."*
*Luke 2:19*

*I will remember the deeds of the LORD; yes, I will remember your miracles of long ago. I will consider all your works and meditate on all your mighty deeds.*
*Psalm 77:11-14*

*I remember to think about the many things you did in years gone by.*
*Psalm 143:5-16*

In these pages, you will record ANYTHING that makes you smile! This can be photos, song lyrics, funny little stories, or observations, as well as happy memories from any point in your life. You can also glue in cards, notes, letters, or other little mementos that bring a smile to your face.

This is also the place you will record your memory re-writes. When you use the Metanoia Method to change a memory, write the new memory in these pages. Remember to get specific. Make it good!

# Happy Memory Tip

Schedule time with a friend or family member. Set the expectations for this meeting before getting together. Tell the other person that you are going to meet up and ONLY share 3-5 of your happiest memories with each other. The other rule is that there can be NO negativity or partially happy memories.

*Example: "I have a great memory of sitting on my grandfathers lap and sharing homemade toffee while we watched The Wizard of Oz. But then he died the next day!!!"*

Nope! Only the good stuff. Remember to use emotion languaging when you are sharing your memories. "It made me feel loved and protected", "I was overcome with joy", "It made me think that I could do anything and feel invincible."

# SMILES

# SMILES

# SMILES

# SMILES

# SMILES

# SMILES

# SMILES

# Smiles

# SAFE HAVEN

*"He takes me to lush pastures. He leads me to refreshing water. He restores my strength. He leads me down the right paths for the sake of his reputation."*
*Psalm 23:2-3*

*For he will hide me in his shelter in the day of trouble; he will conceal me under the cover of his tent; he will lift me high upon a rock.*
*Psalm 27:5 ESV*

*Then they cried to the Lord in their trouble, and he delivered them from their distress. He made the storm be still, and the waves of the sea were hushed. Then they were glad that the waters were quiet, and he brought them to their desired haven. Let them thank the Lord for his steadfast love, for his wondrous works to the children of man!*
*Psalm 107:28-31 ESV*

Anyone who has experienced trauma of any kind can likely explain the importance of "feeling safe" in any given situation. For people who have spent any extended period of time in a "flight/fight/freeze" response, finding a calm, safe environment can be a key to healing. I believe that God knows that feeling safe is an important (if not vital) part of our ability to obey. Over and over in the Bible, we see that God creates places of rest, safety, and respite for His people. We have the power and ability to create these places in our own mind.

For this exercise, we capitalize on the knowledge that our mind doesn't know the difference between "happening now" and "already happened" if we are deeply rehearsing the memory. Having a "safe haven" that we can visit anytime, anywhere, is a valuable tool.

This exercise will be easier for some than others, but I encourage you to keep working on it.

Remember to include all of the sensory categories. SEE it clearly. Use the incredible imagination God has given you. Make all the colors brighter and the images sharper. FEEL it deeply. Practice feeling all the wonderful feelings of being in your "safe place." In mine, I can *feel* the warmth of the sun on my skin and the sand in my toes. HEAR it clearly. Listen for the peaceful tones and all the little sounds that go along with your visions. KNOW what this place evokes in your mind. What are the mantras that repeat in your mind as you are in this place. "I am safe," "I am loved," "I am at peace." One of mine is, "I have nothing to do, nowhere to be, and I'm free to stay as long as I like." If you would also like to add SMELLS (like the salt air) and TASTES that are pleasing and joyful, do it! This is YOUR place, make it the best it can be.

And yes... you can have more than one!! We've left you plenty of room.

## SAFE HAVEN TIP

Many people have asked about having other people in your Safe Haven. My advice is to make sure it is somewhere you feel completely peaceful alone... then you can invite others in when you feel like it! Feeling peaceful and fulfilled when we are alone with ourselves is a valuable and needed skill.

# SAFE HAVEN

# SAFE HAVEN

# Safe Haven

# SAFE HAVEN

# SAFE HAVEN

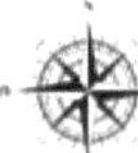

# SAFE HAVEN

# PaNE CuRe

## Past Negative Experiences & Current Realities

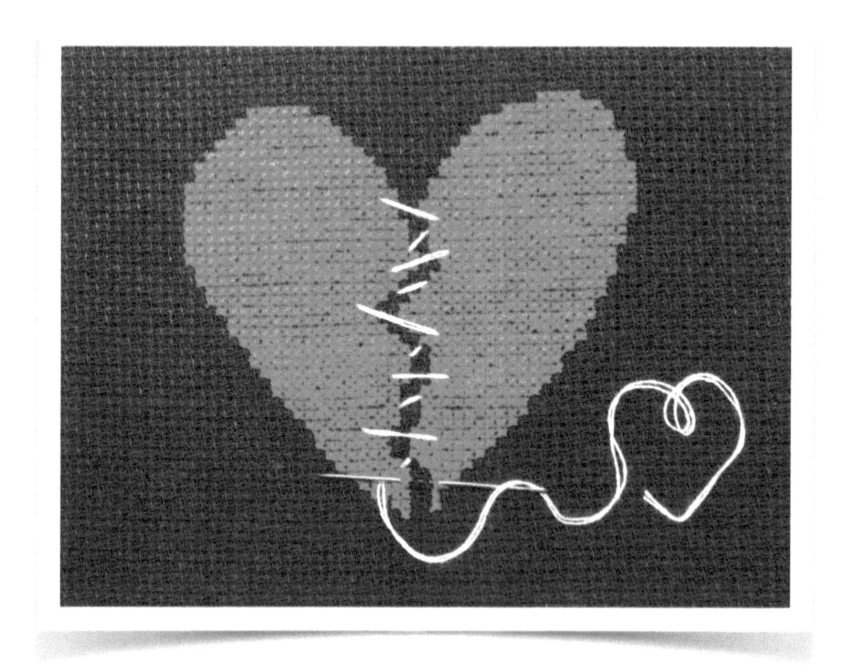

This is a powerful tool that will help you identify the past negative experiences, limiting beliefs, and subconscious programs that are keeping you stuck in some of your unpleasant patterns. It's time to go back and take inventory of the beliefs, memories, and experiences that helped you become who you are right now.

*"Above all else, guard your heart, for everything you do flows from it."*
*Proverbs 4:23*

We have become experts at not dealing with trauma. Instead, we "cope." We often equate "not feeling it" or "not thinking about it" as dealing with something. If it doesn't bother me, it doesn't exist. The problem is that it doesn't bother us because we don't acknowledge it; the "it" is the unpleasant feelings, experiences, thoughts, or past.

Consciously, we can avoid thinking about those negative experiences. But subconsciously, they are alive and well and usually gaining momentum. Remember, it's our subconscious that dictates our daily thoughts, attitudes, and behaviors. It's automatic — the inevitable out-put of what we have input over time.

Unfortunately, no amount of positive thought, positive affirmations, yoga, drugs, booze, sex, or makeup can cover these up forever. Some of these things seem to help, even for long periods. But it always shows up somewhere. As much as we would like to keep "the past in the past," if there are PNEs that need to be processed and resolved, they will keep showing up in different areas of our life.

With the Metanoia Method, we don't run from the past. We don't talk about it until you are tired of hearing about it. We don't ignore it, and we certainly don't judge it. We heal it! Well, technically, YOU heal it with the help of the amazing mind God has given you... we simply facilitate the process.

You may experience a range of emotions when considering this task. Some people are very excited, knowing that identifying the "building blocks" of our experiences, beliefs, and realities is the first step in changing them. Others may feel like this task is daunting. Please give yourself ample time to finish the list.

You do not have to do it all in one sitting. Please give yourself a specific time frame each day that you will work on it. You may find that you desire to continue after the allotted time. That's fine—keep going until you are finished or feel ready to stop for the day. Otherwise, work on it for 10, 20, 30, or 60 minutes, and then stop. Pick it back up the next day.

There will be a temptation to be very emotionally involved in this list. As you are writing the list, it is crucial to remember THIS IS NOT HAPPENING NOW. You are safe. Take this opportunity to learn to be an observer. Yes, these things happened, and you have many thoughts, feelings, and sensations surrounding them. We will deal with all of that. But for now, we are merely recording them for future use.

Also, this would be an excellent time to have your Metanoia Method GPS handy. If, at any point, you feel that you are becoming emotionally "triggered" by making the list, take a break, and look at your GPS. Alternatively, have some funny YouTube videos handy. Whatever makes you uncontrollably happy!

# Making The List

Now you are ready to make your list. Prepare yourself to do this by first sitting down and taking ten deep breaths. Breathing in through your nose and out through your mouth, try to match your inhale to a three-count beat (breathing in for three counts) and exhaling to a four-count beat. When you have completed your breathing, take a moment to invite your subconscious mind to bring forth the information that is needed. You can do this by verbally or mentally acknowledging that you are providing a safe and loving space for this process. Some find it helpful to invite the Holy Spirit to reveal anything that needs healing. When you are ready, you may record this information on the pages that follow.

Starting from birth, or before that, if applicable, list every PNE (perceived negative experience) in your life. You will give the memory a short title and then list 2-3 emotions, feelings, or sensations generated by this memory. You will also rate the emotional intensity of this memory next to the title using a scale of 0-10. 0 being you feel nothing and 10 being the worst feeling, as if it's happening now.

*Below are detailed instructions on getting started:*

## List any pre-birth or ancestral trauma

These will be stories you were told, or family identities. Stories about parents or grandparents, aunts or uncles. Anything that you remember that was an unpleasant trait or story from your ancestry. You may have developed pictures in your mind or have audio recordings of the stories you were told (even if you were not even born yet.). This can even be stories about the kind of people your ancestors were, or your grandparents, or parents. If adopted, list any known or suspected circumstances of the birth parents.

**Example**: My grandfather was a holocaust survivor.

Title the memory, give it a rating and list any related feelings, emotions or physical sensations associated.

- Holocaust stories: (8) fear, anger, rejection

## List any birth stories

This will be stories around your birth or conception that you perceive as negative. Difficult labors, hardships, difficulty of mom getting pregnant.

**Example:**

Mother nearly died in labor: (6) shame, blame, fear

## Chronologically list all other PNEs

It may be helpful to divide your life into time periods (0-5 years old, 6-10 years old, etc.). Consider each time period and try to list 10 or more events. If you remember a specific event but do not have an emotional intensity with it, list it anyway. Title the memory, give it a rating, and list any related feelings, emotions, or physical sensations associated.

## List all Current Realities or Core Beliefs

This will be all the negative and/or unproductive things you believe about your life now. Mantras, negative affirmations, negative "voice in your head", irrational worries, reoccurring dreams, etc.

# List any "Unmentionables"

These will be things that you feel are too difficult to deal with, things you have never told anyone, family secrets, or things that you aren't sure really happened. For these, the titles can be unrelated. For example, someone who remembers an incest incident but has never talked about it could list that event here with a title of "Lemonade". Lemonade may have something or nothing to do with the actual event, but serves as a title for this particular memory.

If you suspect something happened to you, but you have no memory of it, you can make-up a short version of what might have happened and then title it. You don't have to have a conscious construct of a memory to change it. Your subconscious mind already knows.

**Buried traumas that are very sensitive in nature may require the assistance of a trained professional (incest, ritual abuse, extreme physical/sexual abuse). Please don't attempt this on your own, especially if you find a good deal of emotional charge.*

# Events to Include and Consider

- Ancestral Identities/Stories: Wars, cultural tragedies, hardships, etc.
- How siblings & family members felt about you, how they treated you
- School experiences: bullying, shaming, embarrassments, nicknames
- Any sexual abuse or molestation
- First sexual experience: pornography, experimenting, photos/movies
- Emotional or physical abuse
- Religious traumas
- Major moves, changing schools
- Deaths of pets, pet injuries, losses
- Any romantic relationships: especially first boyfriend/girlfriend
- Pivotal points in life with parents, siblings, bosses, co-workers, etc.
- Divorce, relationship breakups, broken friendships, grief & loss: Deaths, loss of job, loss of health, loss of identity
- All hurts: anything you felt bad about when it happened
- All major medical illnesses, chronic illnesses, other medical problems
- Accidents & injuries
- Fears/Phobias: list each experience to support the fear
- Re-occurring beliefs or mantras: "You're not good enough", "You'll never amount to anything", "You are stupid", "I'm always broke", etc.

# Limiting Beliefs

Next is a list of common limiting beliefs (also known as negative cognitions) that people have. The counterpart list of positive beliefs or affirmations can be found in the GPS section. You may want to circle any relevant beliefs to add to your PaNE CuRe. Remember, these are only suggestions. We encourage you to dig deep and see which beliefs fit your model of thinking.

## SELF DEFECTIVENESS

I DON'T DESERVE LOVE

I AM TERRIBLE

I AM SHAMEFUL

I AM UGLY

I DO NOT DESERVE_____

I AM INSIGNIFICANT

I DESERVE TO DIE

I DON'T BELONG

THERE'S SOMETHING WRONG WITH ME

I AM A BAD PERSON

I AM UNWORTHY

I AM UNLOVABLE

I AM NOT GOOD ENOUGH

I AM STUPID

I DESERVE TO BE MISERABLE

I AM A DISAPPOINTMENT

I WILL ALWAYS BE THIS WAY

I AM PERMANENTLY DAMAGED

## SAFETY/VULNERABILITY

I CANNOT BE TRUSTED

I CANNOT TRUST ANYONE

I CANNOT PROTECT MYSELF

IT'S NOT OK TO SHOW EMOTIONS

PEOPLE TAKE ADVANTAGE OF ME

I CANNOT STAND UP FOR MYSELF

THE WORLD IS AN UNSAFE PLACE

IF I LET IT GO, IT WILL HAPPEN AGAIN

PEOPLE ARE DANGEROUS

PEOPLE WILL USE ME

PEOPLE ARE OUT TO GET ME

I CANNOT TRUST MYSELF

I CANNOT LET IT OUT

I CANNOT TRUST MY JUDGMENT

I AM IN DANGER

VULNERABILITY IS WEAKNESS

## RESPONSIBILITY/POWER

I DID SOMETHING WRONG

I SHOULD HAVE KNOWN BETTER

I SHOULD HAVE DONE SOMETHING

NOBODY UNDERSTANDS MY STORY

SOMEONE HAS TO HELP ME

IT ISN'T FAIR

IF THEY WOULDN'T HAVE ______, I WOULDN'T________

I CAN ONLY CHANGE IF THEY______________

I HAVEN'T HAD THE SAME OPPORTUNITIES AS OTHERS

IT'S ALL UP TO ME

IT'S ALL MY FAULT

IT'S WHO I'VE ALWAYS BEEN

NOBODY SEES ME

NOBODY HEARS ME

## CONTROL/CHOICE

| | |
|---|---|
| I AM NOT IN CONTROL | I AM POWERLESS |
| I AM WEAK | I CANNOT GET WHAT I WANT |
| I AM A FAILURE | I CANNOT SUCCEED |
| I HAVE TO BE PERFECT | I CANNOT STAND IT |
| I AM INADEQUATE | I DON'T UNDERSTAND |
| I DON'T HAVE WHAT IT TAKES | I DON'T HAVE TIME |
| NOTHING EVER WORKS OUT FOR ME | I DON'T HAVE THE MONEY |
| I'VE ALREADY TRIED, AND FAILED | IT'S TOO HARD |

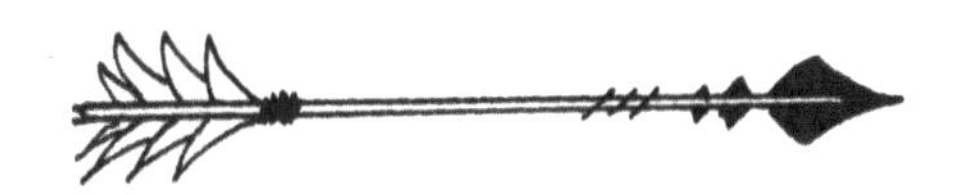

# YOUR PaNE CuRe

Well done digging into these sections! You are almost ready to do the work of Metanoia Method. We have provided a number of sheets for you to work on specific aspects of your PaNE CuRe. When your PaNeCuRe list is ready, have your GPS and Safe Haven close.

# PaNE CuRe

(PRE-BIRTH OR ANCESTRAL TRAUMA)

# PaNE CuRe

(BIRTH STORIES)

# PaNE CuRe

(Chronological PNEs)

# PaNE CuRe

(Chronological PNEs)

# PaNE CuRe

(Chronological PNEs)

# PaNE CuRe

(Chronological PNEs)

# PaNE CuRe

(Chronological PNEs)

# PANE CURE

## (CHRONOLOGICAL PNES)

# PaNE CuRe

(Limiting Core Beliefs)

# PANE CURE

("UNMENTIONABLES")

# PATTERN INTERRUPT

# Where the Magic Happens

A pattern interrupt is a term that comes from hypnosis and is used in Neuro-Linguistic Programming (NLP). It means to change a person's state, pattern, or trance by interruption. A pattern can be interrupted by any unexpected or sudden movement or response. Unless you actively engage your conscious awareness, you will have an almost automatic response to most situations. Our experiences program these responses. When you Pattern Interrupt someone, they experience momentary confusion, and in some circumstances, transient amnesia. This confusion state can make you open to suggestion. We can program in another state of mind within these moments. Not only that, but with enough "interruption," we can completely scramble a well-known program, pathway, or trance.

The information feedback loop between our brain and body works very similarly to the encoding of a CD. If we understand the cyclical nature of that loop, we can use it to our advantage. When we are in an undesirable loop, we can interrupt it, like scratching a CD. Do it enough times, and it won't play any longer!

I think Jesus used this technique in a well-known story. In John 8, we meet the "adulterous woman." If you are a little rusty on the details, I encourage you to read it again. At the height of the tension, when the Pharisees and the teachers of the Law are formally accusing the woman of adultery before Jesus, he does a very curious thing—he bends down and begins to write on the ground. What?! Why on earth would he do such a thing? I want you to imagine this crowd of people standing around, watching this debacle. Who do you think they were looking at most? Who had everyone's focus? The woman, standing there in shame, likely nude or at least in some state of undress. What do you think happened when Jesus suddenly bent to the ground and began writing on it with his finger? This was an epic pattern interrupt! All eyes were on him now, and for a brief moment, the attention and focus were completely off the woman and her shame. Coincidence? I think not. How do I know? He does it again a few minutes later! I love Jesus for this. Not only does he not want this woman to be publicly humiliated for her transgression (even though she was clearly in a sinful situation), he even cares about her accusers.

Jesus first pulls the focus off the woman (immersed in her guilt and shame), and then pulls it to himself and the ground. With this break in the narrative, he capitalizes on the way the human brain works and provides some perspective. He then stands up again and redirects all that shame and blame, transforming it into a question straight back to the ones who were dishing it out. He puts the ball back in their courts, involving every listener and watcher there. But even then, Jesus doesn't want people to wallow in any shame or blame.

So he drops to the ground again and resumes his writing. With this second break in focus, this powerful and unexpected digression from the norm, Jesus is mercifully offering another chance at perspective. It is an ingenious move that is loving but firm. It is full of conviction and mercy, simultaneously. Have you ever considered that there was more behind what seemed like such an odd move from Jesus? Can you see it clearly now?

Pattern interrupts have been used, knowingly and unknowingly, for centuries. It's time for us to learn to harness this God-given tool. With a little practice and a little time, you will come to see how powerful it can be for you and for those around you.

# Trance

A little more on the "trance" concept. We are in a trance the majority of the time. With an average of up to 50,000 thoughts per day, up to 95% of those thoughts are the same thoughts we had yesterday. We then repeat those same thoughts over and over again, every day. That's a lot of practice! These have all been categorized and now are nearly automatic productions. Driving to work: Trance. Performing your work duties: Trance. Speaking with coworkers: Trance. It's the "How" you do things. Your brain already "knows how" because it does it, in some form or fashion, every day.

This is why it can seem so hard to change at times. We are keeping ourselves in the same situations, thinking the same thoughts, producing the same feelings day after day. We have a conscious awareness that we would like to be different, but we use the same resources to produce a different result. That is rarely successful. If we can be aware of these programs and make conscious efforts to interrupt those repetitive messages, then we are left open to suggestions. The brain has to recalibrate because you are introducing something unknown and unexpected into the feedback loop. Since we already have our Metanoia Manifesto, we can always suggest something in alignment with what we want for the future!

# Types of Pattern Interrupts

There are countless types of Pattern Interrupts to help you change your mind. Next, I will list some examples in conjunction with each common Representational System. Used in conjunction with the other concepts, tools, and suggestions in this book, a Pattern Interrupt is an incredibly powerful tool. Remember, this is far more than just a distraction. This is an intentional effort to interrupt and corrupt any line of negative thinking. Some will work better than others. Find what works for you!

# Visual Pattern Interrupts

- Watch a funny YouTube video
- Look through your GPS
- See the memory on an Etch-A-Sketch and slide the bar to erase
- Open your eyes and do figure 8 patterns with your eyes
- Push the image so far away in your mind, you can no longer see it
- Picture Jesus sitting or standing next to you with you with his arm gently on your shoulder
- See the memory as a photo in your mind, now adjust the color until it's all white
- See the memory as a photo, now put it into a magicians hat, snap your fingers, and watch it disappear. Look back in the hat and see what good thing has arrived to replace it
- See all the memories you need to work on as laundry around a room. Collect each item and put it into a laundry basket. Now, do the wash. See how differently the memories come out of the wash
- Picture yourself casting all your anxiety onto Jesus
- Envision everyone in the memory dressed as Disney princesses. How does this change things?
- Envision everyone in the memory as if they were penguins. How does this change things?
- Envision everyone in the memory with their underwear on the outside of their clothes. How does this change things?
- Put the memory on a photo and then create another photo next to it. In this photo, create the perfect scenario. Now, overlay the "good" scenario on top of the old photo. Watch the old photo fade away
- Envision your hero showing up in the memory. How would they have changed it?
- Try to envision what it would look like to see two elephants ice-skating in pink tutus
- Try to envision two porcupines slow dancing while wearing cowboy boots
- Open your eyes and count all the blue items in your surroundings
- Open your eyes and blink along to the tune of Twinkle, Twinkle

# Auditory Pattern Interrupts

- Listen to a favorite song
- Sing the SpongeBob Squarepants theme
- Speak the lyrics to a nursery rhyme
- Play a noise (fart, baby laughing, animal sounds)
- Hear what your hero or loved one would say to you instead.
- Hear the ocean waves
- If you are hearing someone say words to you that are negative, change their voice to your favorite cartoon character
- Say, "I release and let go of the power I have given this memory"
- Play the words that someone is speaking to you in the memory in reverse
- Hear the Holy Spirit whisper in your ear your favorite bible verse
- Quote your favorite movie
- Take a deep breath in and breathe out slowly with an "S" sound the whole time, making it as loud as you can
- Make beatbox sounds and try to keep the beat
- Imagine you are popping bubble wrap. What does it sound like?
- Remember back to the first time you heard your favorite song and notice the volume and turn it up!
- Do your best impression of Kermit the frog and Miss Piggy
- Imagine there was a mute button on a negative memory. How would this change your feelings?
- Imagine your song playing in reverse
- Shout at the top of your lungs, "I am more than enough!"
- Do the Darth Vader heavy breathing voice and say "Luke, I am your father"
- Put your wrist up to your ear and listen to your pulse beating
- Gulp some water down as LOUD as you can
- Whisper "I'm safe now"

# Kinesthetic Pattern Interrupts

- Stand up and turn around before sitting back down
- Do 5-10 jumping jacks / push-ups / pull-ups / squats
- Balance for 10 seconds on one foot touching your head with your fingers
- Clap your hands 13 minus 6 times
- Snap your fingers to the beat of "Let it go"
- Try and move your eyebrows up and down individually
- Give yourself a shoulder rub
- Give yourself the biggest hug possible and imagine it's Santa
- Do a little dance in the mirror

# Audio-Digital Pattern Interrupts

- Imagine that the conversation in your mind is being had with another (higher level) you. What insight does the other "you" have?
- What is the overall message of this memory? Notice it and write it down. Is this thought or belief one that you want more of? What would you rather believe?
- If this memory were a person, who would it be?
- If this memory had a belief what would it be?
- Can you list 3 things that might contradict the message of this memory?
- What message does the Holy Spirit have for you about this experience?

** Audio/Digital representation is when we are "in our own head". It involves having a dialogue or conversation with yourself about the situation. The most helpful thing will be to step back and become aware of the conversation. Do what you need to interrupt the voice in your head.

**You are ready to begin Metanoia Method!**

Next is a review of the basic Metanoia Method process, followed by a section you can use as you begin changing specific memories and beliefs. Most people have about 10-15 core memories that drive them to do what they do not want to do. When you shift your perception of those core memories, your entire world shifts.

## THE METANOIA METHOD PROCESS

Now, think about or recall the problem or event in detail. Notice the emotions, feelings, sounds, and/or specific images that are present in this memory. Allow it to happen as if it's happening RIGHT NOW. If it's safe to do so, step into the memory, imagine yourself really there, see what you saw, hear what you heard, and feel what you felt. This is the time to make it as strong as possible because it will only last a short amount of time. This should take you no longer than 30 seconds to 1 minute. Any longer and you begin *practicing* the feelings all over again, because the feedback loop has already been playing.

As soon as you reach this place, it's time to open your eyes and engage a **Pattern Interrupt**. The optimal Pattern Interrupt will be one that corresponds with the Representational System that you used to most fully recall this memory. For instance, if you have a mental picture of the memory (V), open your eyes and look through your GPS. Or, you can visit your mental Safe Haven. Alternatively, you can watch a quick YouTube video of funny animals. Spend 30 seconds or so in any one or more of these activities. The most important thing is to shift your focus completely from the memory (picture, feeling, sensation, sound) you are working on, to the Pattern Interrupt.

As soon as you are ready, close your eyes and take 2 deep breaths (3-4 second inhales through the nose, followed by 4-5 second exhales through the mouth). Notice that breathing brings you back to a grounded place. Now, go back and check your memory that you are working on. Notice what has changed. Notice that the intensity has lessened, or the picture has changed. Maybe the feeling has reduced or moved to another part of your body. Just notice what's left. Now, go to any part of the memory that still bothers you, notice how you know it bothers you, intensify it if you can, see what you see/feel/hear... now, Pattern Interrupt again.

# RATING YOUR MEMORY

Once you've identified HOW you know this event happened, notice how much it bothers you. Now you can give the memory a rating to acknowledge how much it bothers you. Something like, on a scale of 0-10, 0 being you feel nothing at all and 10 you feel as if this is happening again right now, how much can you make this memory bother you? Write this number down beside the title on your paper.

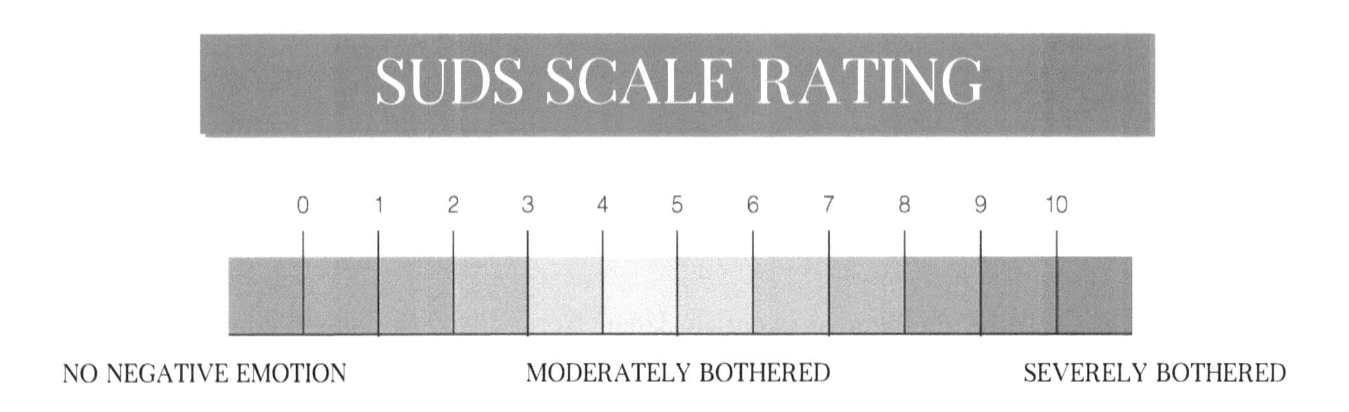


This will be easier for some than others. That is okay. If you have a difficult time finding an accurate number, just make a guess. We ask you to rate your memories as a guide to show you the progress that is being made.

If you find that the number goes "UP" while you are working on the memory, this means that you have amplified or found additional resources to support this memory. It doesn't mean it's "getting worse." It simply means that your subconscious mind is digging up all the ways that this memory bothered you. Just notice any additional information that may arise and let it go. As the intensity of the memory decreases, notice that you are able to begin to experience the memory in a different way now.

Pictures may change. The audio may disappear or lessen. The feelings may dissipate or change to something more peaceful.

Continue to change your rating as you move through the process. Until you reach "0" (Zero). Meaning that the memory no longer bothers you . At that point, you are ready for the next step!

# KEEP GOING UNTIL IT'S GREAT

Continue this process until the memory can no longer bother you. Once you can no longer make the memory bother you, it's time to change your mind. If the memory was primarily a picture, you may notice that the picture has already changed. The brain is amazing that way! If not, you may just notice that you can no longer find the picture, or it has gone blurry. Now is the time to be intentional about what we hold within. Ask yourself, "What would I have rather seen instead?" If auditory, "What would I have rather heard?" If kinesthetic, "What would I have rather felt?" Make it good, because you will get more of what you hold! Go back into the memory and re-decorate a bit.

If you are working on a memory and find resistance, that is okay. It doesn't mean it didn't work, it only means you have a little more investment in this belief. It may be foundational and could require one or two sessions of self work. Take a break and come back later. You may find that the memory is now changed. If not, you will likely find less resistance when you revisit it. Just think, it probably took you many years to develop such a deeply-rooted response. Or you have practiced this memory thousands of times, therefore reinforcing it daily. It may take you a few hours or even days to re-write some of these events, but it is well worth it!

**A word of caution: Though this method has been used to tackle some of the most devastating traumas, it is advised that you work with a skilled practitioner if you find that the emotional charge of the memory is too high. The trance of the painful memory can sometimes be so powerful that you have a very difficult time breaking it on your own. This is where an experienced professional can utilize different protocols to break that trance. This is very deep work and it can be very beneficial to work with someone who has been trained to handle any situation that may arise.*

*It is the ultimate goal of any Mind Change practitioner to empower the client to work on themselves eventually. So starting out with a practitioner can be very beneficial.*

*For those of you interested in scheduling sessions, learning more, taking any number of online courses, or becoming an associate practitioner, please visit the website at www.MindChange.com for more information.*

# A COUPLE MORE THINGS

As you are working through your list, you may encounter some "bumps" in the road. That is totally normal, and to be expected. Here are a couple of things that might show up.

## Secondary Gains

*"One who was there had been an invalid for thirty-eight years. When Jesus saw him lying there and learned that he had been in this condition for a long time, he asked him, 'Do you want to get well?'"*
*John 5:5-6*

These are any subconscious "benefits" of our problems that keep our limiting beliefs in place. Remember, these typically don't "make sense" to us on a conscious level. But the subconscious mind makes these logical connections from our past, based on experience.

**Example #1**: When I have a migraine, people don't expect me to do anything. So I finally get that break I need so badly.

**Example #2:** When I am overweight, I don't attract male attention. Therefore I am safe from unwanted advances.

**Example #3**: I have already failed so many times, I will probably do it again. So if I sabotage this great job opportunity *now*, I won't have to suffer the humiliation of a larger failure down the road.

Remember, the goal of your subconscious mind is to keep you safe. If we can identify some of the potential benefits, or secondary gains within a limiting belief, we can train our subconscious minds that it's safe to do something else.

# Resistance

It is common to find resistance whenever you attempt to change beliefs. If you find resistance, that is okay. It can even be good. Resistance is a good indicator of investment. It is good to see what beliefs you are really invested in.

Resistance can show up in many different ways.

- Lack of motivation to work on yourself
- Memories refusing to change
- Getting sleepy, sick, or agitated when you begin to work
- Not being able to "find" the memories
- Overcomplicating the Metanoia Method process
- Not making the time to do the work
- And more....

If you find resistance, there are a few ways to handle it:

- You can acknowledge it as resistance, thank it for coming (as a safety mechanism) and mentally include it in what you are working on.
- You can work on the resistance *before* moving on. Just use the same process for the resistance as you would for a memory. When you are finished, just go back to the memory you were originally working with.
- You can acknowledge it, thank it for showing up to protect you, and then just jot it down to deal with at a later time. Often times, just acknowledging the resistance will be enough to move past it.

Remember, it is there to "keep you safe". But that doesn't mean we need to keep doing things the same way.

On the pages to follow, we give you an example of a Metanoia Method Worksheet followed by blank worksheets for you to fill out and work through. This is a sample only. If it works for you, great! If you find another format that is a better fit, that is okay too. On the first example, you will see the worksheet filled out with the "problem". On the second example, you will find the same worksheet, but with the results listed as well. Again, these are just examples to get you started.

# THE METANOIA METHOD IN ACTION

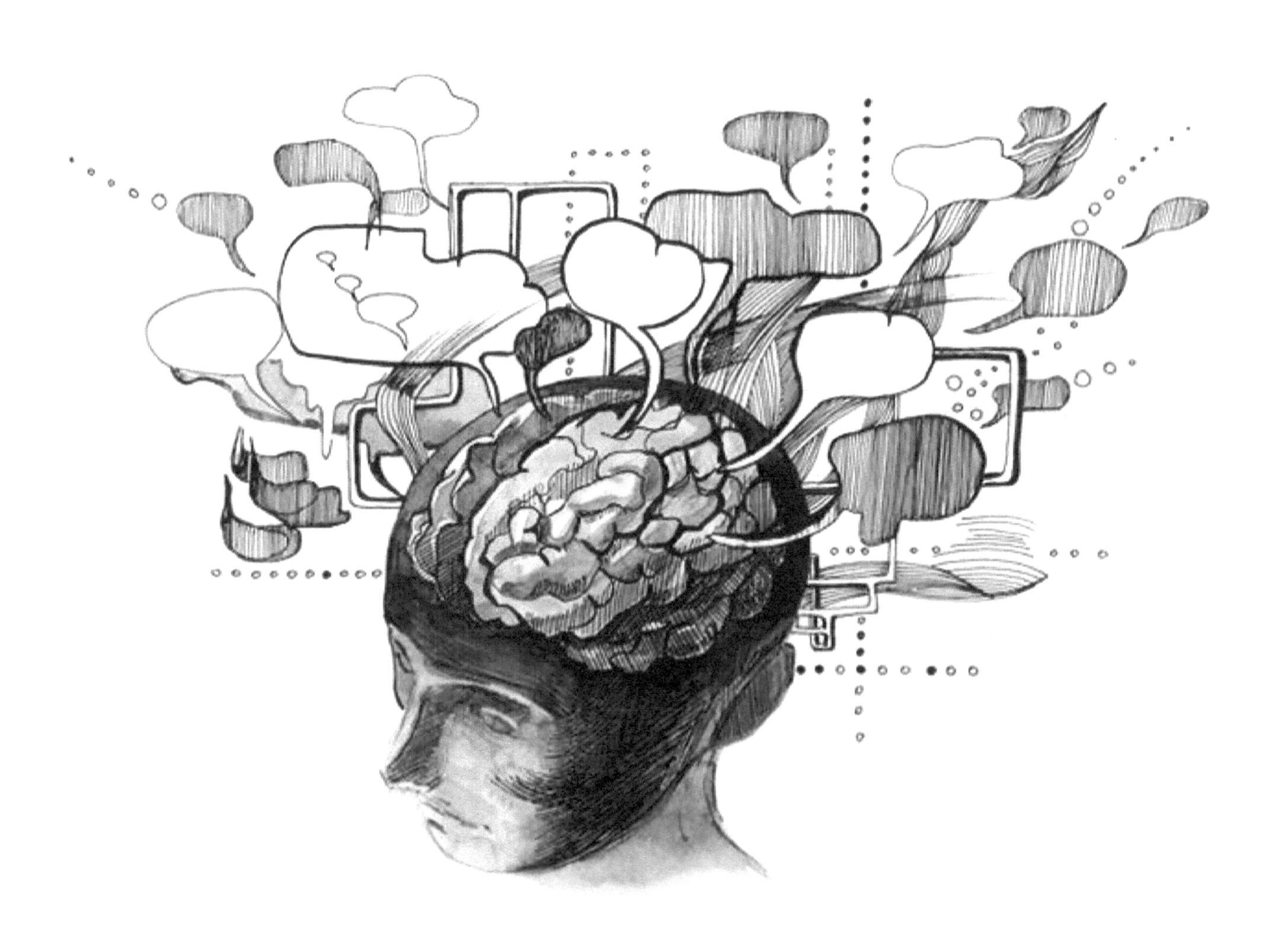

# EXAMPLE (PART 1)

| MEMORY TITLE: | | | | |
|---|---|---|---|---|
| **HOW** (V, A, K, O, G, A/D) | **BULLET POINTS** | **RATING:** | **How I changed it!** (Write this in your GPS) | **Most Effective Pattern Interrupt Used** |
| **V** | • I can see myself on the ground with the other kids around me<br>• I can see their angry faces<br>• I can see tears streaming down my face and dirt on my clothes<br>• I see the color of the blood dripping from my nose | 8 | | |
| **K** | • I feel mad, hurt, scared, embarrassed, full of rage, wanting revenge<br>• I feel the anger of the other children | 10 | | |
| **A** | • I hear them shouting "Fight, Fight"<br>• I hear laughing, shouting and the sound of the blood pumping through my body<br>• I hear my short, fast breaths | 7 | | |
| **O** | • I could smell the dirt and my sweat | 2 | | |
| **G** | — | — | | |
| **A/D** | • I believed I was weak<br>• I did something wrong<br>• People dont like me<br>• I need protect myself<br>• People are unsafe<br>• Nobody protected me | 7 | | |

# EXAMPLE (PART 2)

| MEMORY TITLE: | | | | |
|---|---|---|---|---|
| **HOW** (V, A, K, O, G, A/D) | **BULLET POINTS** | **RATING:** | **How I changed it!** (Write this in your GPS) | **Most Effective Pattern Interrupt Used** |
| **V** | • I can see myself on the ground with the other kids around me<br>• I can see their angry faces<br>• I can see tears streaming down my face and dirt on my clothes<br>• I see the color of the blood dripping from my nose | 8 | I now see me and the group of friends playing Red Rover all together. We are all smiling, having fun, and free. We love and support each other. | Looking through my GPS |
| **K** | • I feel mad, hurt, scared, embarrassed, full of rage, wanting revenge<br>• I feel the anger of the other children | 10 | I feel free and supported. The other children feel loved and supported as well. We all are grateful for the friendships that we have and feel safe to play. | Jumping Jacks |
| **A** | • I hear them shouting "Fight, Fight"<br>• I hear laughing, shouting, and the sound of the blood pumping through my body<br>• I hear my short, fast breaths | 7 | I hear all of us laughing and yelling, "Red Rover, Red Rover, let Suzie come over!"<br>I hear encouragement from all the friends. | Listening to a Baby Laughing |
| **O** | • I could smell the dirt and my sweat | 2 | I smell lollipops and popcorn | Visiting my Safe Haven |
| **G** | — | — | | |
| **A/D** | • I believed I was weak<br>• I did something wrong<br>• People dont like me<br>• I need protect myself<br>• People are unsafe<br>• Nobody protected me | 7 | This day I learned that I easily fit in and am loved<br>I am such a good friend<br>Friends are good and fun<br>I am safe and protected | Repeating my positive affirmation out loud |

## Choosing A Memory

Either chronologically, by intensity or perceived importance, pick a memory or problem to work on. If it is a problem, take a minute to notice how you know it's a problem. Allow any pictures, feelings, or sensations to surface. You may notice that one or more memories surface. If so, notate those. Even if you think they are unrelated, just trust the subconscious mind and work through what comes up.

Write the title of this memory down (on the pages to follow). Close your eyes and GO THERE. Notice what you notice. HOW do you know this happened? Do you see pictures? Hear voices or words? Does a feeling emerge? Maybe it's a mixture of one or more. The most important part of this is knowing HOW you know.

**It is important NOT to spend a great deal of time here, trying to "figure it out". Just notice HOW you know and then move on. If you find that you cannot answer "How do I know?", then just put it as a "knowing". But the more visual/kinesthetic/auditory details that you can notice, the quicker you can begin to change it.*

### Under the memory title, write one of the following letters:

**V:** If you are seeing pictures, movies or snapshots, write V (Visual) on your paper next to the title.

**A:** If you are hearing things within the memory, write A (Auditory) on your paper next to the title.

**K:** If you have feelings, sensations or emotions arise, write K (Kinesthetic) on your paper next to the title.

**O:** If you have smells in this memory, write O (Olfactory) on your paper next to the title.

**G:** If you have tastes that arise, write G (Gustatory) on your paper next to the title.

**A/D:** If you have an internal dialogue that you can hear or a" knowing" that it happened but nothing else, write A/D (Audio Digital) on your paper next to the title. These can also be beliefs that you developed about yourself.

(Note: you may have one or more ways you are holding this memory. Just notate all that apply).

For each letter that applied to you, write 2-3 different things you notice from that category.

## Working Through Your PaNE CuRe List

Prepare yourself for each session by taking a moment of prayer or meditation and/or breathing, using this time to give thanks for the ability to do this work and for the healing that will happen. Next, choose a calm, quiet area where you will not be disturbed. Set a timer for the amount of time you would like to spend.

If you have your Safe Haven handy, this would be a great time to go there and spend a minute or so indulging in the good feelings. As you do this, engage in some deep breathing. Deep, 3-4 second inhales through the nose, followed by 4-5 second exhales through the mouth. Do this 4-5 times or until your "feel good" state is achieved.

## IT'S TIME TO GET STARTED

You are ready. It's time. In the beginning, this will be unfamiliar and "clunky". Keep working at it. It gets easier. Learning to change your mind is a skill. The more you practice, the better you get.

Let's be the adventurers of our own destiny, the surveyors of our own mind. Let us make friends with our subconscious mind and begin to learn the language of our souls. If you need help, reach out. Read more. Listen more. Become an expert in the art of YOU.

We suggest that you use the following worksheets to begin to address some of the memories on your PaNE CuRe list. Beyond that, feel free to utilize the same format in the examples, or explore other options that may work for you.

Remember to FIRST fill in the "How," "Bullet Points," and "Rating." Then, after you have worked on yourself using the Metanoia Method, fill out "How I changed it!" and the "Most Effective Pattern Interrupt Used."

In order to help you along the way, please feel free to check out our YouTube Channel and enter this unlisted video as a bonus for those who have purchased this handbook — This video is a live demonstration of how to work on yourself (please type it into your browser bar exactly as it is shown here):

<u>https://youtu.be/0dGNbKqi5o8</u>

## Helpful Metanoia Method Questions To Ask Yourself

Below are a list of questions that can help you identify different aspects of the PNE in order to fully clear out the problem and change it. If you get stuck, these are great to run through to let your subconscious answer on a deeper level. Do not think about the answer before answering. Whatever comes up first is the best place to start. The final two questions can be used after you have cleaned up the issue in order to change that old story into a new and wonderful one.

- How do I know I have this problem?
- What do I believe about this problem?
- What is the worst part about this problem?
- When did this begin?
- What else was going on when this started?
- When was the first time I remember having this problem?
- Who else do I know that has this problem?
- What happens inside me when I have this problem?
- What do I see / hear / feel / taste / smell / know?
- If this was a person, who would it be?
- If this had a voice what would it say?
- If this had a message, what would it be?
- What would I rather have happened?
- How could I make this even better?

**MEMORY TITLE:**

| HOW (V, A, K, O, G, A/D) | BULLET POINTS | RATING: | How I changed it! (Write this in your GPS) | Most Effective Pattern Interrupt Used |
|---|---|---|---|---|
| V | | | | |
| K | | | | |
| A | | | | |
| O | | | | |
| G | | | | |
| A/D | | | | |

## MEMORY TITLE:

| HOW (V, A, K, O, G, A/D) | BULLET POINTS | RATING: | How I changed it! (Write this in your GPS) | Most Effective Pattern Interrupt Used |
|---|---|---|---|---|
| V | | | | |
| K | | | | |
| A | | | | |
| O | | | | |
| G | | | | |
| A/D | | | | |

**MEMORY TITLE:**

| HOW (V, A, K, O, G, A/D) | BULLET POINTS | RATING: | How I changed it! (Write this in your GPS) | Most Effective Pattern Interrupt Used |
|---|---|---|---|---|
| V | | | | |
| K | | | | |
| A | | | | |
| O | | | | |
| G | | | | |
| A/D | | | | |

## MEMORY TITLE:

| HOW (V, A, K, O, G, A/D) | BULLET POINTS | RATING: | How I changed it! (Write this in your GPS) | Most Effective Pattern Interrupt Used |
|---|---|---|---|---|
| V | | | | |
| K | | | | |
| A | | | | |
| O | | | | |
| G | | | | |
| A/D | | | | |

**MEMORY TITLE:**

| HOW (V, A, K, O, G, A/D) | BULLET POINTS | RATING: | How I changed it! (Write this in your GPS) | Most Effective Pattern Interrupt Used |
|---|---|---|---|---|
| **V** | | | | |
| **K** | | | | |
| **A** | | | | |
| **O** | | | | |
| **G** | | | | |
| **A/D** | | | | |

**MEMORY TITLE:**

| HOW (V, A, K, O, G, A/D) | BULLET POINTS | RATING: | How I changed it! (Write this in your GPS) | Most Effective Pattern Interrupt Used |
|---|---|---|---|---|
| V | | | | |
| K | | | | |
| A | | | | |
| O | | | | |
| G | | | | |
| A/D | | | | |

**MEMORY TITLE:**

| HOW (V, A, K, O, G, A/D) | BULLET POINTS | RATING: | How I changed it! (Write this in your GPS) | Most Effective Pattern Interrupt Used |
|---|---|---|---|---|
| V | | | | |
| K | | | | |
| A | | | | |
| O | | | | |
| G | | | | |
| A/D | | | | |

## MEMORY TITLE:

| HOW (V, A, K, O, G, A/D) | BULLET POINTS | RATING: | How I changed it! (Write this in your GPS) | Most Effective Pattern Interrupt Used |
|---|---|---|---|---|
| V | | | | |
| K | | | | |
| A | | | | |
| O | | | | |
| G | | | | |
| A/D | | | | |

| MEMORY TITLE: | | | | |
|---|---|---|---|---|
| **HOW** (V, A, K, O, G, A/D) | **BULLET POINTS** | **RATING:** | **How I changed it!** (Write this in your GPS) | **Most Effective Pattern Interrupt Used** |
| **V** | | | | |
| **K** | | | | |
| **A** | | | | |
| **O** | | | | |
| **G** | | | | |
| **A/D** | | | | |

| MEMORY TITLE: | | | | |
|---|---|---|---|---|
| **HOW** (V, A, K, O, G, A/D) | **BULLET POINTS** | **RATING:** | **How I changed it!** (Write this in your GPS) | **Most Effective Pattern Interrupt Used** |
| **V** | | | | |
| **K** | | | | |
| **A** | | | | |
| **O** | | | | |
| **G** | | | | |
| **A/D** | | | | |

**MEMORY TITLE:**

| HOW (V, A, K, O, G, A/D) | BULLET POINTS | RATING: | How I changed it! (Write this in your GPS) | Most Effective Pattern Interrupt Used |
|---|---|---|---|---|
| V | | | | |
| K | | | | |
| A | | | | |
| O | | | | |
| G | | | | |
| A/D | | | | |

| MEMORY TITLE: | | | | |
|---|---|---|---|---|
| **HOW** (V, A, K, O, G, A/D) | **BULLET POINTS** | **RATING:** | **How I changed it!** (Write this in your GPS) | **Most Effective Pattern Interrupt Used** |
| **V** | | | | |
| **K** | | | | |
| **A** | | | | |
| **O** | | | | |
| **G** | | | | |
| **A/D** | | | | |

**MEMORY TITLE:**

| HOW (V, A, K, O, G, A/D) | BULLET POINTS | RATING: | How I changed it! (Write this in your GPS) | Most Effective Pattern Interrupt Used |
|---|---|---|---|---|
| V | | | | |
| K | | | | |
| A | | | | |
| O | | | | |
| G | | | | |
| A/D | | | | |

# BONUS

# ReWrite Your Childhood

What if you were able to see everything in your past and childhood from a lens of love? This is a little bonus section that can be extremely powerful for your life. Our childhoods have a profound effect on our current behaviors and realties. Some people may balk at this exercise, thinking that our past is "in our past" and cannot be changed. I found this to be untrue. For me, I was so focused on the negative memories that I was holding on to, that I had neglected the majority of the positive memories. When I cleared up many of those negative references, I was free to experience my childhood in a completely different way.

If memory is... unreliable at best, it's safe to say that a large portion of our past had already been changed. Our repeated accessing of those memories, by our perceptions as we mature, and by the particular events we choose to focus on. So if most of our past is "made-up" anyway, shouldn't we make-it-up in a good way? If you are going to tell yourself stories (especially if they have a direct effect on your current behavior), make sure you are telling yourself good ones!!

This is your chance to rewrite the "childhood of your dreams". Like the question in the Manifesto section, this is a chance to elaborate on how good things would be if everyone in your life as a child was living from their higher self.

If you find resistance to this, add that to your PaNE CuRe list and work it out! Allow your parents the opportunity to parent in the best way possible. Allow your siblings to be as supportive and encouraging they could be. If you were an only child, let that be a great experience for you in every way.

If there is anyone in your immediate family, or close family that you need to make peace with, clean that up in your PaNE CuRe list and let them live their best self HERE in your story.

Some of you had great childhoods, and that is wonderful! Write out all the amazing reasons why! Could it have been EVEN BETTER?!? Write that story too. Don't hold back. The "little you" deserves every good thing. Go back and set that child free!

*Jesus said, "Let the little children come to me, and do not hinder them, for the kingdom of heaven belongs to such as these."*

*Matthew 19:14*

# READY, SET, GO!!!

# Congratulations!

Well Done! You did it! This is another step in the journey to your BEST LIFE. Come on — admit it… you are even more awesome than before. Am I right? You have just added incredibly powerful tools to your "toolbox of life" that will continue to empower you throughout your journey. Keep doing the work. We are never really done. Life keeps happening, so we need to keep being intentional about creating it. If this handbook is full, get another one! Or make your own. Just keep them going.

Share this with others! We would love to see a photo of you with your journal. Post a picture on social media and tag us **@MetanoiaMethod** — Spread the love and encouragement. Goodness knows the world needs as much hope, change, and positivity as it can get.

Thank you for investing in YOU. Thank you for doing the work and healing the past hurts in your life. Don't worry if there are more. You have the power to change it now. You are now clearer on who you are, what you want to create in life, and the direction you want to go in. We are sending you lots of light, love, and peace on the next stage of your path. Keep us in the loop!

May many more successes and victories be yours.
Aloha and Peace,

The Metanoia Method Team

Made in United States
Troutdale, OR
09/05/2023